T0197402

M. J. COLE

PAPILLON

Butterflies are Like Me

AuthorHouse™
1663 Liberty Drive
Bloomington, IN 47403
www.authorhouse.com
Phone: 833-262-8899

Because of the dynamic nature of the Internet, any web addresses or links contained in this book may have changed since publication and may no longer be valid. The views expressed in this work are solely those of the author and do not necessarily reflect the views of the publisher, and the publisher hereby disclaims any responsibility for them.

Any people depicted in stock imagery provided by Getty Images are models, and such images are being used for illustrative purposes only.
Certain stock imagery © Getty Images.

This book is printed on acid-free paper.

ISBN: 978-1-6655-3281-5 (sc)
ISBN: 978-1-6655-3282-2 (e)

Print information available on the last page.

Published by AuthorHouse 07/23/2021

authorHOUSE

This is a Blue Mountain blossomed adult with its brilliant blue. We strut our stuff in the things that we do.

Butterflies are like you and me.

They come with wiggles and eat constantly.

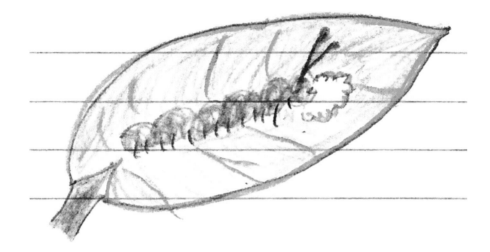

All butterflies eat and grow.

They began to explore.

They eat and eat and eat some more.

They crawl around with a limited view,

without knowing the things full grown

butterflies do.

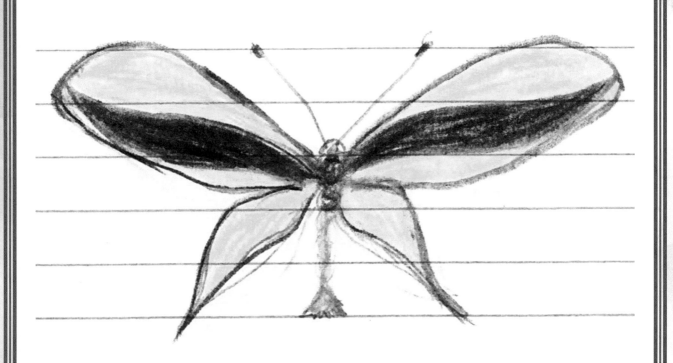

This is a Tailed Birdwing fellow. His large wings flutter with brilliant yellow.

Butterflies taste different things until they find what they like;
Then, that's all they want day and night.

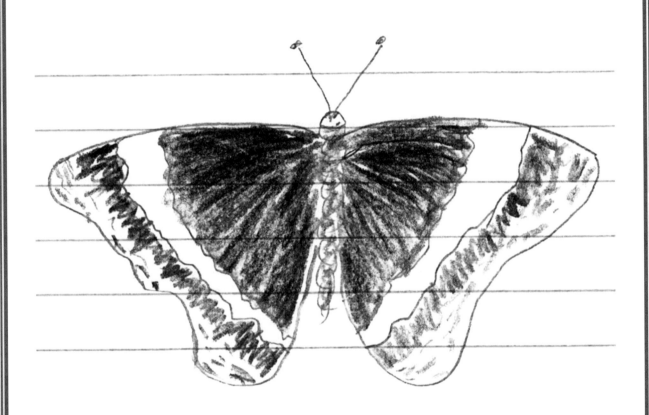

The White Admiral is another, with its distinguishing black and white. Its wings are also outstanding when it takes flight.

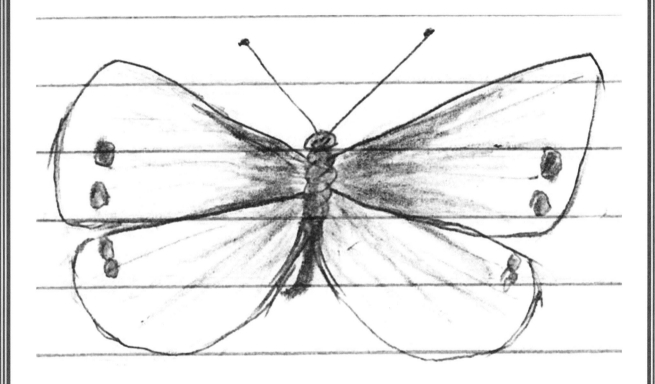

The Cabbage butterfly is among the flock. This beauty certainly is not new on the block.

These beauties grow and discover, and grow and discover...

until it's time for them to take cover.

They begin to change. Oh, this change takes

little time. When they emerge from their

enclosed shrine...

no longer looking up to the world, like when

they first came; no – things are different

now – nothing's the same.

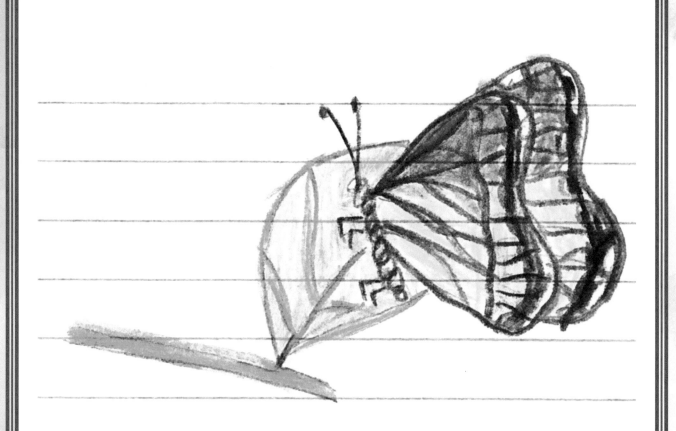

The Monarch Butterfly is best known of all. They come to the South when the season turns fall. They fly to and fro looking to feed; South to North laying eggs and seeking milkweed.

The life cycle is a process we all know, children all around post it for show. They lay eggs first, you see, then next they are born larvae. Caterpillar is what the larvae goes by. The eating machines are working as they lie. From leaf to leaf and over again, the creatures eat as much as they can.

They then begin to pupate. That's when they change from state to state. This stage may last two weeks or a whole winter. The completed process is the hinter. Then the emergent has powdered, colorful scales that gives it a brilliance that never pales. This process continues to repeat, you see; so we can witness a beauty that flies free.

Printed in the United States
by Baker & Taylor Publisher Services